HOW GREEN
IS YOUR
GRASS

A Book Of
Poems

Contents

The call

The world
watched a
president
today.

I watched my
president
today.

Standing tall.
Talking
strong. His
eyes wide and
true—a novel
experience.
His face
weathered by
time. His
smile shows
his soul.

A man with
wisdom and
courage.

A man who has
seen a lot. A
man who holds

our future in
his hands.

A man who
holds the
future of a
country in his
hands.

A country
inflamed by
hatred, lies,
and deceit.

A country hot,
yet frigid,
fighting
against
itself.

I don't trust
a lot. I don't
love a lot,
but I trust
this man. I
love this man
filled with
promises,
filled with
hope.

This man
hardened by
experience and

wisdom, and
yes,
frailties.

He has felt
and seen a
lot. He has
lost and
gained a lot.

Like a mighty
oak
withstanding
and
weathering, he
stands tall.

He stands tall
with the
burden of a
country in
tatters to be
fixed by a man
of age, a man
of God.

He promises
with
conviction and
we listen.

He promises
and we trust.

This man of
faith, this
man of
convictions.
So many
convictions.

Shoulders not
slumped. Face
weathered by
time,
experience,
and hurt.

He headed the
call, our
call. Steeped
in his faith,
he knew he had
to answer.

Stately and
presidential,
he stands by
us—ready to
mend the
broken fences,
broken
relationships.

He tries. He
mends.

A mad bull ran
through our
lives,
shattering our
dreams and our
hopes for a
better
tomorrow for
our children
and their
children. It
left us
bewildered,
dejected. He
saw that, this
man of faith,
this man of
God.

Now we listen
to the
speeches of
and music of
the greats.
Our hearts are
open again;
our hopes are
high again.

This man of
God, this man
of faith. This

man whose
smiles light
the way for
us. This
president.

Our lives
matter

With hatred,
jealousy, and
abhorrence, he
lay his knee
on the man's
neck, ignoring
his plea for
mercy, his cry
for leniency.
The cry for
his life.

Once again the
cry for mercy
gurgled in
Joe's throat
as he ached
(that could be
you or me). He
committed no
crimes. He was
a black man. A
man of color,
man with no
wealth.

Wrong color,
wrong place,

wrong time.
But was it
wrong place
and time or
just wrong
color? He
gurgled his
last breath
yet the knee
still pressed
as if pulling
death from the
dead.
Unconscionable
Dead inside.

A storm is
coming. They
didn't know
it. They
didn't care.

A storm of
color with
mixed cry for
justice—
justice for
the man of
color with the
knee on his
neck. Justice
for all people

of color with
white knees on
their necks.

Balled fist
raised. Angry
voices echo
the cry of
Joe. "Take
your knee off
my neck."

Voices raised,
calling for
the injustice
to stop, the
killing of our
children and
grandchildren
to stop.

Born of
slavery. How
much more
blood do you
want? How much
more blood has
to be shed to
secure our
place in
society, to
secure our
place among

the human
race? Our
race. Take
your knee off
my neck.

Too much, too
long. We've
suffered long
enough at the
brutality and
hostility of
those supposed
to protect us
from the
brutality and
hostility.

We try to
forgive, but
they won't let
us forget that
no matter how
hard we try,
there's
prejudice and
jealousy and
malice and
divide among
us.

With bullets,
they kill us.

With pepper
spray, they
try to blind
us from seeing
the truth of
their own
maligned ways,
the truth of
their
ugliness.

We push back
peacefully,
still the call
for justice.
Take your knee
off my neck.

An ocean of
color,
marching,
calling for
those in
charge to
speak, to
command. The
silence is
deafening. The
injustice is
frightening,
yet we march
with balled

fists raised
high in anger
and disgust.
Black lives
matter.

People of
color
shouting, "Our
lives matter."
We are a part
of the human
race. One
race,
indivisible.
One nation.
One God. One
life. One
truth. One
justice for
all. Still,
they keep
their knees on
our necks.
Trying to
stifle us.
Trying to
silence us.
Trying to kill
us.
Accountability

Take your knee
off my neck.
My life
matters. I am
somebody. I am
human. Open
our eyes, open
your heart.
Our lives
matter.

Lies

I guarded you.
I stood up for
you. I tried
to keep you
safe, keep
your secrets,
to keep your
integrity
intact.

In one fell
swoop, you
decimated me
with an
ejaculation of
lies and
deception.

You didn't
talk of your
own impotence,
your own
frailty. You
didn't talk of
all the
degrading
things you
said and did
to me. You

fell right
into being
yourself, who
you are and
always will
be—a liar, a
cheat, a
whoremonger. A
person
incapable of
taking
responsibility
for his own
actions, his
own frailties.

You bring me
down to build
you up because
that's all you
are capable
of, no matter
what.

Nothing I do
is ever right.
You pull and
pull and push
and push. My
unhappiness is
your
happiness.

My downfall is
your
uplifting.

I see the
abhorrence in
your eyes,
your face,
your heart,
your stance. I
see the
abhorrence in
your heart,
your soul,
causing
distrust.
Disappointed,
disillusioned.

Trampled and
cast aside
like a woman
who had not
once mopped
your vomit and
witnessed your
betrayal
firsthand.

Are we there yet

I don't know
what happened
way back when,
other than
what I read in
history books,
literature.

But I wonder,
Are we there
yet?

I see the
faces—mouth
agape,
laughing, eyes
open wide. I
wonder, Is
this the new
times, the new
age when we
accept without
question? When
we forget our
history?

I know there
was whipping,
bloodshed,
indecencies,
flesh open,
bleeding, no
favors
granted.

I close my
eyes, and I
can hear the
screams as if
it was just
yesterday. I
see the bloody
backs of
blacks—an
array of
color,
suffering,
bawling for
mercy, though
there was
none.

Are we there
yet?

It was all for
us now. Can't
we see the
suffering they

23

bore was all
for us to be
free, to live,
to love, free
to be who we
want to be,
free to live
our lives the
way we see
fit.

The blood they
shed was so
we'd keep
ours.

They hid to
read so that
we can
articulate
their strife.

We no longer
have to hide,
but to be
educated to
the highest
level.

Are we there
yet? Can we
feel it? Can
you taste it?

We are there,
so grab hold
and never let
go of your
piece of the
cloud,
peaceful now.
Don't let it
all be in
vain; it's
yours.

We're there,
and not a drop
of blood
should be
spilled; it
was already
shed for us.

The spoken word

The spoken
word is like
the wind on a
hot summer's
day, welcomed
with
appreciation,
welcomed with
love, fanning
your face like
romance in the
evening's
light.

A word like
the wind can
never be
withdrawn.

A word like
the wind can
never be
returned.

The spoken
word is like
the wind on a

frigid
winter's
night, harsh
and cruel like
a slap across
the face from
an angry
lover.

A word like
the wind on a
cheery spring
day can make
your heart
soar, can make
your spirit
fly.

A word like a
tornado can
sweep you
across the
skies, can
lift you to
heaven's door.

A word like
the wind can
make your
tears fall
like rain or
your mouth
laugh like a

field of
tulips.

Be careful of
the spoken
word. It can
mend a broken
heart or rip
it wide open
like a sharp
sword on a
body, rending
it from head
to toe.

Call me

When the dust
from the air
finally
settles to the
ground never
more to rise,
call me. When
the rivers run
upstream and a
pebble dropped
in a pond does
not expand,
call me. When
the ocean lays
quiet and the
sand
undrenched
moves no more,
call me.

When the wind
blows no more
and the birds
refuse to fly,
call me.

When the
earth's axis

slows to a
halt, call me.

When the
heavens no
longer open
their doors
and the rain
falls no more,
call me.

When the skies
turn bright
red and all
the clouds
vanish from
above our
heads and the
flowers dry
and wither,
look behind
you. I've
always been
there for you.
Just touch me.

The little things

Through life's
ups and downs,
we learn to
identify the
emotions that
will befall us
and the ones
that will keep
us safe. But
we often
ignore and
push aside the
downs,
trusting the
ups will stay
and keep us
warm. The ups
will outweigh
the downs.
That is often
a lie, a cop-
out because we
don't want to
face the
reality of the
downs.

Through our
denials, we
suffer at the
hands of those
so close to us
who become
complacent
with our
attitude of
silence,
mistaking it
for
acceptance.

We are really
not that
complicated,
but they try
to make us so,
to question
our own
achievements,
our own worth.
In their
laziness, they
lump us all
together, not
knowing how to
take the time
to know us.

They further
dig in to tear
us down, to
make us feel
unworthy, to
lift
themselves up
through
falsehood and
lies.

While we
believe the
lie and try to
work harder to
be our true
selves, they
work equally
as hard to
tear us down.

Our
unhappiness is
their
happiness,
though
falsely, you
wonder why.
What
satisfaction
can a man
achieve by

making another
miserable?
Power over
you? Lauding
over you?
Trying to keep
you
subservient?
Knowing that
your
intelligence
will always be
unmatched by
him. Until he
can admit his
faults like
you can admit
your faults,
he will never
and can never
be happy, and
the downs will
always be
down.

Move on. See
the light and
the positivity
in yourself.
Seek truth and
happiness
elsewhere. Do

not allow your
joy to be
stolen. Do not
allow your
thunder to be
silenced. Do
not hide your
intelligence,
who you are
under a
smokeless
fire. If you
have no fire,
you have no
warmth, and no
one will see
your signal.
Raise the
temperature;
let them see
your fire.

Unanswered questions

As a child I
walked in the
path you set
for me.

As a teenager
I tried to do
the things
that were
right, and I
very rarely
strayed. Even
when things
got rough and
temptation was
high, I still
remembered the
path and tried
to hide in it.

I became an
adult, and I
know I
strayed, but I
have never
stopped

looking for
the path.

I looked in
churches,
synagogues, in
the streets
and the
forest.

I searched for
your shadow in
the sunshine
and your
silhouette in
the moonlight.

I followed you
as a child.
Then, when I
thought I
could not go
on any longer
and the entire
world was
against me and
man threw away
that
encouraging
word, my soul
ached with
hunger for

your words and
presence.

I took to the
soft sand of
the beach in
search of the
path once set
for me and
found the path
that made my
heart light
and my worries
cease.

Still asking
questions
without
receiving
answers, I
continue
walking,
clearing a
path of my own
but never far
from the one
set for me,
the path that
gave my life
meaning and
purpose.

Once again the
set path faded
as turbulence
hit my life.
Then I looked
up and saw the
fingers of God
in the shape
of a funnel
cloud pointing
to the ocean,
to a whirlwind
that formed
and swirled.

I'm not sure I
understand,
but I
concluded that
you're all
around me. My
path was once
again set. All
doubts
disappeared.
Unanswered
questions were
answered, and
my faith
strengthened.

I'll always be me

I'll be your
rose among
thorns.

I'll be your
water when you
thirst.

I'll even be
your stepping
stone to
success, but
I'll always be
me.

I'll be your
road map when
you lose your
way.

I'll be the
sun to light
your way out
of the
darkness, to
help you see
right from
wrong, to fill

your cup when
you think it's
half-empty,
but you can
never change
me.

Mediocrity

Why do you
work so hard
when the pain
is so great?

Why do you
work so hard
amid so much
frustration?

Always be
prepared for
the worst and
hope for the
best so you'll
be well
prepared to
accept gold
and no less.

Why do you
work so hard
to be the best
when others
lay about and
accept
mediocrity,
where silver

or bronze is
just fine and
envy is the
order of the
day?

Why do others
accept
mediocrity
when you, who
cannot accept
it, are looked
at with scorn?
They wear
smiling faces
but wish they
were you with
all your
integrity and
security of
self.

Is there a
group for you
who work hard
at being the
best, where
mediocrity is
never an
option?

Why do you
work so hard

and still feel
so
unappreciated?

Is there
something
you're
missing, a
game you're
not willing to
play because
your self-
esteem and
intelligence
levels far
exceed those
who accept
mediocrity?

The truth is
always self-
evident. It's
okay to strive
for and
achieve the
gold.

You can't take it from us

Try as you
may, try as
you might, you
cannot turn
back the hands
of time.

Try as you
might, you
cannot unlearn
what has
already been
learned, what
has already
been taught.

But for future
generations,
you act like a
thief in broad
daylight. Come
to steal what
is rightfully
ours,
education.

You want to
steal our
history, our

birthright.
You want to
push it back
into darkness;
you would like
to steal our
light.

You want to
steal what our
foreparents
worked so hard
for—what they
bled and
suffered for,
our education
of their
suffering.

You would like
to place us
under the
sheath of
darkness where
our
foreparents
hid to learn
to read and
write to let
us know about
their
suffering.

You can't stop
us now, from
learning our
history of the
beatings and
degradation at
the hands of
the masses.
The raping,
the beatings,
the hangings.
It's all true,
you know; the
darkness came
to light in
books and
poetry, in the
written and
spoken word.

You cannot
rewrite our
history. What
was done is
done, and from
that we rise.

We rise to
teach, to
learn, to
realize.

We realize
that you
cannot do it
for us. We
have to and
have been
doing it for
ourselves,
driven by
history.

You cannot
take away our
history no
matter how
hard you try.

You may try to
hide our
books, our
literature,
but you cannot
burn them;
those days are
gone.

We'll find
them because
we want to
know our
history. We
want to be
propelled by

our history,
to run. To
rise.

No longer will
we be the
downtrodden.

We will
educate and be
educated.

Try as you
may, try as
you might, we
will prevail.

We have the
right. It
wasn't given
to us; we took
it on the
backs of our
foreparents.

They marched;
their blood
was shed; and
now here we
are, standing
tall. There's
no going back;
there's no
hiding. No

matter how
hard you try,
you cannot
rewrite our
history. We
are here to
stay. We will
not be
invisible.
Look at us, a
proud people
standing tall.

A letter to my mother

Mom, I've
loved you from
my very first
breath. The
very first
moment we
shared. From
the very first
time you held
me in your
arms and
kissed my
face. From the
very first
time I saw
your smile I
grabbed hold
of your finger
with my tiny
hand—my
lifeline.

Infant,
toddler. Thank
you for
picking me up
when I fell,
for kissing my

booboos to
make me feel
better.

Thank you for
holding me
when I cried
and rocking me
when I was
tired.

Thank you for
washing me
when I stomped
in the mud
after a rain
shower.

You seemed
tireless then,
always there.
I never knew
you were tired
when you held
me and rocked
me to sleep
and your own
eyes closed in
sleep.

I loved you
then, and I
love you now.

There is so
much more I
want to say,
but my eyes
are a little
glossy with
tears right
now, Mom.

Mom, I'm sorry
that you hurt
when you hurt.
You did so
much for me.
You sacrificed
so much. You
worked
tirelessly and
hardly
complained.

Mom, you make
me want to
hold my head
so high. I'm
so proud of
your
teachings,
your tender
ways, and your
encouraging
words. Thank

you for taking
the time to
listen when I
called, even
when I rambled
on.

You braved
snowy days and
wintery nights
to be with me,
and I thank
you for that.

You warned me
about the
perils ahead,
and I thank
you for that.

Through you, I
learned to
love and to
trust my
instincts—to
grow and to
appreciate the
little things
in and of
life. To stop
and just take
a breath every

once in a
while.

I see your
eyes, your
smile, your
face before me
every day,
especially
your laughter.
Oh, Mom. I
love you
forever, and I
miss you
always.

You were a
lady in the
true sense of
the word, the
epitome of who
I strive to
be. You walked
with grace and
pride in who
you had
become. A
beacon to
light my way,
strength to
hold me up,
and a love

that only you
could give.
Mother, I love
you.

The children

Anger races
through me
like the
blazing
savannah. No
water to
quench the
flames,
burning and
scorching all
in its path,
devouring all
in its wake.

I turned my
head away, but
the images
were already
ingrained in
my brain.

Nowhere to
turn, no way
to turn off
the sight of
caged
children.
Their tiny
fingers

pressed onto
fences holding
them into
prison, away
from their
loved ones,
away from
their grieving
mothers and
fathers. Their
tear-stained
faces, their
eyes puffy
from constant
tears bleeding
from their
eyes.

They cry out
for their
parents, but
no one hears
their cries.
Their jailors
walk with
batons, heads
held straight
as if ears
stopped.

Children
wrenched from

the breasts of
their mothers
who cry, No!
Please don't
take my child.
They are
turned away.

They look back
at their caged
children,
their hearts
drenched with
pain, their
knees weak
from wanting
to hold their
child one more
time. I can't
look, but I
can't turn
away.

I have a bed
to sleep in;
they do not.
Wrapped in
foil, they
sleep with
their tear-
stained faces
and little

hearts beating
fast, unsure
what tomorrow
will bring
while a
riotous man
sits
unwavering,
uncaring.

I bleed for
the children.
I bleed for
their parents;
there's
nothing I can
do but
understand
their pain.

I have food to
eat. What do
they eat? No
water to wash
their dirty
faces. No
freedom. Caged
like animals.
Their
outstretched
arms meet the
cruel sun, the

humid air.
Sweat drips
from their
faces. No one
hears their
cries—too
many, too
many. No
laughter, just
tears and
heart-
wrenching
sadness while
the fat cat
sits, while
the fat cat
moves on to
things. So
easy for him
to block out
the sounds,
the screaming,
the cries from
babies,
toddlers,
infants caged
like rats. Do
you care?

Do you hear
the mothers
crying for

their
children? For
a better life
they came,
walking for
miles, hoping,
hoping. Hopes
dashed,
smashed like
glass
shattering to
the ground in
tiny
splintering
pieces. Hope
was all they
carried in
their hearts.
Hope that this
great country
would have
pity and hear
their cry for
help. Hope.

Dance with me

Fingers
feathery light
against the
small of my
back, barely
touching, so
magical.

Our bodies
move in sync
like making
love but never
touching.

His moves are
calculated,
learned.
Practiced,
perfect.

As if alone on
a crowded
dance floor,
carried on the
notes of the
song, we move,
owning the
dance floor.
He a stranger,
me, smitten.

Smitten by a
man I've known
forever but
never met.

The heat of
our bodies
melding yet
never
touching,
moving,
gliding like a
whisper in the
dark.

Fluttering
against my
back, his
magical
fingers softly
drum to the
beat of the
music.

Swaying,
gliding,
turning on a
pillow of
clouds.

Take me home,
my mind says.
But you don't

know him, my
mind
rebuttals—this
man of
mysteries,
this man of
pleasure, this
man of warmth
and care. Our
eyes meet and
hold, our lips
so close only
a kiss is
missing.

I could stay
with him in
this dance
forever. Want
to stay in
this dance
with him
forever.

Close the door
to the harsh
reality of
life, safe.

I don't want
to let go, I

must not, I
will not.

Swept up in
sweet rapture,
I close my
eyes.

Our fingertips
so close to
intertwining
yet not
touching.

Then I awake
to the reality
away from my
dream, my
dance.

Westmoreland was grand

A long time
ago, starry-
eyed lovers
walked,
unafraid feet
not touching
the ground.
Amid laughter
of innocence,
time stood
still in
Westmoreland.

Westmoreland
carried all
the voices,
whispering,
"There they
go. Their
love's so
deep, they
haven't a
clue."

Do they know
what they're
getting into?

Hand in hand,
breath of a
child, hearts
on fire.
Westmoreland
was grand in
those days.
Generations
stood in pride
and watched
starry-eyed
lovers, no
riches in
their grasp.
What a laugh
of desire.

Survival was
imminent,
there was no
doubt, and
into gray
they'd go and
come back to
Westmoreland
once more to
visit the
beginning so
long ago.

Those days
were grand,

unspoiled not
by jealousy or
pomposity.
Just plain
country folk
up to their
eyeballs in
love.

Westmoreland
was grand,
babies all
grown.
Generations
have come with
flying doves
and growing
wealth at
hand, laughing
from
innocence.

Westmoreland
was grand for
country folk
like them.
They made it a
long time ago,
starry-eyed
lovers walking
barefoot
blazed the

path into
tomorrow's
light.

Oh, what a
wonderful
place,
Westmoreland
grand.

Heal

How do we heal
after the loss
of a loved one
taken too
soon, too
soon.

We band
together
through tears
and holding.
We remember
the good
times. We
remember the
good times.

Let go of the
bad times;
she's gone to
heaven now. No
tears for her.
No more
hurting for
her. Just
peace, just
love.

How do we
heal? We

remember,
carry them in
our hearts
forever. No
one can take
away the
memories.

It's ok to
cry. It's ok
to curl up in
bed with her
memories, but
not too long
because you
have to rise
and go on with
your own life.
She would want
you to.

Remember she's
always in your
heart.
Remember the
smiles, the
laughter.

I know, gone
too soon, but
God always has
a plan. Only
he knows why.

We heal. We go
on holding
them in our
hearts. They
would want it
that way. Go
on, heal.

The nature of things

Beauty
surrounds us
yet we cannot
see it.

We are so
filled with
hate and
prejudgment
that our minds
are clogged.
We don't have
the impetus to
think clearly,
to make clear
and justified
decisions.

Music
surrounds us,
yet we cannot
hear it. We
cannot feel
the vibrations
of the
instruments.
We cannot hear

or understand
the ballads.

It could be
the trickling
of a stream or
the sound of a
roaring
waterfall.

It could be
the call of
the wild,
birds singing,
chirping,
squawking.

It's all music
if you know
how to listen.

Beauty is not
just within
the petals of
a flower, but
deep within
where the
nectar
resides.

We are
consumed with
hate because
we don't

understand or
we don't take
the time to
listen and
understand.

It's not just
the words, but
what the words
mean. Look
deep, listen
well, and you
may just learn
something.

Unrecognizable faces in a crowd

I stand here
before you
telling you I
love you, yet
I don't want
to know you.

You're just
empty faces in
a crowd ready
to do my
bidding.

I will never
sup with you
or invite you
into my inner
circle. To me,
you're just
blank faces in
a crowd—no
names, no
personality.
You mean
nothing to me.
But...

Go, plunder
and pillage.

Destroy that
which is held
so sacred.

Steal, lie for
me, but you're
just blank
faces in a
crowd. You
mean nothing
to me.

Kill for me,
but I will
deny you
because you're
just blank
faces in a
crowd willing
to follow me.
Willing to
fall face-
first into an
abys while I
stand by and
watch safely
from a
distance.

And they went.
They pillaged,
destroyed, and
killed all in
my name. I
denied every
word I spoke
to them. I
stood by,
satisfied,
laughing while
they paid the
price for me.
They were just
blank faces in
a crowd.

I would not
die for them;
I would not be
jailed for
them.

I denied the
commands I
made; I do
not love them.
I only love
myself, and to
me they are
just blank

faces in a
crowd.

Oh, such fools
you are. Do
you really
believe all my
lies? Yes, you
do; otherwise
you would not
shout my name
like the
antichrist I
think I am.

Love

I love you, I
thought, not
wanting to say
it out loud.
Once I say it,
I cannot take
it back.
Looking like a
fool, I stare,
anticipating a
positive
response.

What will
happen if I
say it out
loud?

Will it come
back to me in
kind?

I don't know.

Must I? Might
I take a
chance? I'm
afraid.

Are you afraid
to say those

words,
thinking I
don't or won't
reciprocate?

We are both
afraid it will
never be said.

We will never
know.

Maybe, just
maybe actions
will play a
part. Ahh,
yes, you do
love me.

Yes, I love
you.

Sometimes
words are
unnecessary
when actions
are strong and
convey.

The past

Did I wrong
you in another
life? A life I
can't recall.

Did I make you
unhappy, the
way you've
vowed to make
my life a
living hell?

Was I a
vehicle for
your dismay or
your jealousy?

Was it a
recent life,
one you seem
to remember so
well?

What did I do,
pray tell?

For you,
happiness must

be fleeting
for me.

Laughter, a
swift slap
across the
face and it's
gone, the way
you like it
just for me.
Did I wrong
you in another
life?

Were we
enemies? Was I
someone else's
lover,
bringing your
jealousy to a
boil because
you couldn't
have me then,
and now that
you have me,
it's revenge
that you seek?

What was I in
the other
life, your
conscience,
because now

you're my
nemesis, my
only enemy?

Maybe I love
you in this
life. Aren't
we supposed to
learn from the
past?

Must I again
reflect on
this life in
the next life
to see if I've
wronged you in
another life?

Nature at work

Every time I
see nature in
movement, I'm
amazed.

A rainfall or
a storm.

The steady
flow of water,
trillions of
tiny droplets
descending,
and as heavy
as water gets,
the wind can
always push it
around. Isn't
that amazing?

A windstorm
can move a
mighty ocean,
uproot the
strongest
tree, whip a
jetliner out
of the skies,
and gently

sway a tiny
baby's rocker.

Gentle breeze
allows a small
bird to glide
happily along
its merry way.

Every time I
see a bird, I
marvel—whether
it's in flight
or sitting
still. Their
colors of
bright orange,
green, black,
blue, white,
brown and
multicolor—I
could go on,
but wouldn't
you rather see
them for
yourself?

Birds sing so
sweetly, so
melodiously,
so distinctly
from one
another.

Some in
groups, some a
couple, some
just loners
going through
life like you
and me.

Some mate for
life unlike
some of us.

Nature made
waterfalls.
Ice caps
forming, ice
caps melting.

Creatures of
the sea still
with their
songs, mating
or just
because.

Fly fish,
jumping fish.
Giant mammals
gliding along
living their
lives. I could
go on, but
wouldn't you

rather witness
it for
yourself?

Mother nature
in motion—what
a sight to
see.

Revere

Branches
swaying.
Leaves
dancing. Water
gently
rippling by.
Ducks wading
in the stream.
Birds flapping
their wings,
seemingly so
quiet.

I close my
eyes, not to
block out the
serene sights
but to reflect
on my life.
I've tried to
live right. I
don't follow,
neither do I
stride to
lead. The
burden of
leadership is
daunting. Not
all, including

myself, want
to be led. I
make decisions
that propel my
life in a
spiritual way.
Don't cheat.

Try not to
lie.

Try to uplift
others.

Try to listen
rather than
force my
opinion on
others.

My life only
seems to be in
tatters right
now, but I'm
strong. I will
rise again.

I will,
however, allow
myself this
time of
weakness to
cry. To be
angry. To

break down. To
rebuild. To
turn my
weakness into
strength and
try my utmost
not to make
the same
mistakes
twice.

A house made
of straw will
easily blow
away with
chatter, and
then come
lies,
jealousy, and
misinformation

Build a house
of brick;
build a house
of truth.
Choose your
friends very
carefully, and
don't sweat
the small
stuff.

Dear diary

It is not for
me to speak of
my importance.

It is not for
me to speak of
my beauty, my
courage, or my
feats because
I don't know
how important
I am or if
what I'm doing
is that
important or
necessary to
the life
around me.

It is not for
you to feel my
importance, or
my beauty, to
allow it to
make your life
better or
brighter.

I don't know
of my own
beauty. I can
only see it
through your
eyes.

My courage I
get from deep
within.

I sit like a
crow or a dove
sometimes on a
bending
branch, hoping
it won't break
and I won't
fall.

I try to keep
things in
perspective,
though
sometimes it's
hard and I get
tired, but I
never forget
that I have
the right to
speak my mind.
To love and to
appreciate

free art and
laughter, and
oh yes, the
art of
bitching—never
let that go. I
always
exercise the
art of
bitching.

I never forget
to stand for
what I believe
in. I make
sure you know
my beliefs.

I never forget
to be fully
dressed when I
criticize
someone who's
half dressed.

When I die, I
want to leave
something
behind that
people can
appreciate.
I'll get back

to you on that
one.

I'm never
afraid to talk
about my
blackness, to
appreciate my
blackness
because I
cannot change,
and if I
could, I'd
never want to
change that
which is so
beautiful and
glorious. That
which
surrounds and
protects me
always. I
never forget
where I'm
coming from,
and I know
where I aspire
to go.

I'm open to
all things,
but I'm very

selective in
what I do, who
I associate
with, and whom
I
metaphorically
lay with
because when
it's all said
and done, the
face that
looks back at
me from behind
the mirror is
always mine.

Woman's world

Women, they're
headstrong,
purposeful,
powerful,
angry…
sometimes.

Willful,
sometimes.

Forceful, most
times.

Loving, most
times.

Graceful,
sometimes.

Romantic, we
want to be.

Gentle, we
must.

We can't be
everything to
everyone all
the time.

Yes, we're
strong; we
have to be to
bear the
children, to
raise the
children.
We're mother
to all.

Awesome.

Angry, yes. We
cannot laugh
all the time;
neither can we
cry all the
time. No,
we're not
angry all the
time, but when
we become
angry, watch
out.

We cannot
stand the
killing, the
raping. The
massacring of
our children,
our land, our
pride.

Forceful, uh
huh. We have
to protect
ourselves in
so many ways
in order to
protect future
generations,
the leaders of
the free
world.

Do not dismay,
my friends;
this is not
politics.

Yes, I do
believe that
one day all
the world will
be free. After
all, I am
woman. I know.

Ahh, the
loving side.
The side that
makes us
graceful.

The side that
brings us pain

and suffering
because woman
don't only
bear women.
Women bear
men.

And not only
do we bear
men, we love
men, hence the
pain.

But sometimes
it's okay
because we
complement
each other.

One's no good
without the
other, or are
they?

The gentle
side; what can
I say, we've
got it.

God's greatest creation

God created
woman with
natural
instincts.

God created
woman to bear
man, to build
man, to
comfort man,
to strengthen
man, to soothe
man.

To lift man
when he's
down. To
comfort man
when his world
falls apart.

God built
woman's
fragile
shoulders
strong and
unbending so

that man can
lay on it and
tell her his
troubles while
she soothes
him with sweet
words of
encouragement.

God built
woman's arms
to enfold man
and fingers to
wipe away his
tears should
he choose to
shed them.

God gave woman
eyes so that
she could see,
and see she
did.

She saw all
that man did
and all that
he was.

She read his
lying lips and
his cheating
heart.

Woman was sad.

This is not
the man she
tended.

This is not
the man she
soothed and
comforted.

Where is that
man? What is
this man? Then
God gave woman
heart, and man
shattered it
into tiny
pieces.

Black and sweet

Gimme a cup of
coffee. Black,
real strong.

Gimme a cup of
cream, real
sweet, thick
cream.

Gimme a cup of
sugar. The
darker the
coffee, the
sweeter the
sugar.

Pour the cream
into the black
coffee, a
little at a
time. Mix
well.

Add sugar—
dark, sweet
sugar—a little
at a time. Mix
it all

together very
slowly, really
well.

Look at it,
take a sip,
savor it.

A cup of real
sweet, dark
coffee. Drop
in a bit of
chocolate, add
brown eyes and
luscious
cherry lips,
and you've got
the woman of
your dreams.
Don't blow it!

Woman

Woman, you've
come of age.

Woman, you've
come alive.

Out of the
background,
out of the
shadows.

You've emerged
to strength.
You've emerged
to heights.

Without claims
and without
brawl, but
with brains,
determination,
and savvy.

You've
realized
power. You've
embraced
power, but the

soft side
never leaves.

There are no
roars. There
is no
boasting.

You've gently
broken down
and pushed
away the
barriers that
kept you
behind.

You stride
through
barriers with
grace and
panache.

You walk into
life with
shoulders of
strength.

You hold the
scalpel of
life with
trust and
certainty.

You impart
knowledge of
times long
past.

You wear a hat
of steel and
fly jet liners
with
confidence.

You've been to
the moon and
back, and that
tender side
still
prevails.

You cry, you
laugh, you
hurt.

You are woman.
You're
nature's
perfect seed.
God's greatest
creation.

Dare I say

Love is not
holding onto
or controlling
but letting go
to fly and
search and
encourage.
Love is never
angry.

Love is never
jealous of
one's
achievements
but revels in
the
satisfaction
of that
achievement.

Love is all
encompassing,
all
surrounding.

Love is that
one thing that
is never

planned but
smiles where
anger once
was. It's a
pat on the
back, a peck
on the cheek.

Love is
soothing, a
feeling that
sometimes
escapes or
defies
predictions,
an
explanation.
It's adoring
and
compelling.

Love is the
purest human
emotion that
can turn
deadly and
deeply
regretful.

Love is not
robust or
obstructive

but plain and
sticky sweet.

Love is
attending a
chick flick or
an action
movie with
your
significant
other when you
could be off
doing
something with
the boys/girls
in the street.

Love is
compromising
and always
finding a way
together.

It's holding
hands and
stealing
kisses in a
crowded room
of boring
executives—
example, old
bankers and
politicians.

Love is love,
and dare I say
tender moments
of giggling
and gazing
into each
other's eyes
and being shy
or trembling
at the touch
of a hand or
having sweaty
palms. Dare I
say again…
pits. Love is
mushy.

Love is you
and me hand in
hand on a
moonlit night,
walking on the
beach,
skipping the
waves and
laughing,
carefree.

Love is love,
what can I
say.

The heart

The heart is
the hardest
thing to
govern, for it
betrays with
emotions that
cry out for
release.

It is not
opposed to
betrayal of
the body and
mind as they
grow old and
weary. Love
withers while
pain tears at
the heart, but
no, death does
not come when
love is lost,
even when we
beg for its
presence to
torture us.

God help us,
for it is only
on our knees
with heads
bowed,
surrendered
that the heart
is governed
and healed. No
barriers shall
we construct
against the
heart. For
once again, it
must love so
that we may
dance and
laugh. And
yes, even cry,
for it's a
journey that
must continue.

My wife

Give me a man
who loves so
deeply that he
would sell his
very soul for
the woman he
promised to
love and
cherish for
the rest of
his life.

Give me a man
who respects
so earnestly
that he would
never lie to
his woman,
never slander
his woman,
never
embarrass his
woman, never
bear false
witness
against his

woman. His
wife.

Give me a man
who would
never allow
another to
embarrass his
woman with
words that he
has spoken or
by his own
actions.

Give me a man
who would
never use his
woman to gain
favor or save
face.

Give me a man
whose love is
unconditional.
Will never
look at
another woman
with lust or
wanting.

Give me a man
who loves
deeply every

day of his life. Respects earnestly and would give anything and everything for the happiness of his wife. Give me a real man who feels deeply and loves with all his heart. A man whose entire world revolves around the woman he loves. His wife.

Come Home

Wings that are
tired of
fluttering.

Arms that
unfurl, then
coil to
embrace.

Fluttering
wings above
the clouds
drew you
closer when
the Lord saw
you tire.

You did so
much for so
many.

You loved
completely.

You were
strong and
independent,
but as your
fluttering
wings became
tired, the
Lord said,
"You've done
enough; come
home."

On an angel's
wings, you
flew into arms
unfurled.

Into the arms
of the only
One who gave
you love, the
only love you
deserved
without
hesitation.

To say we will
miss you, my
sister, is an
understatement

To say we will
miss, you dear
mother, is an
understatement
Your smile,
your laughter,
your strength,
your faith
will remain
with us
always.

Goodbye, my
friend, my
mother, my
sister. Until
we meet again
in that great
beyond.

You really can't go home again

I never really
believed that
I could not go
home again.

I didn't
really know
the true
meaning of the
words, "You
can't go home
again."

Why can't I go
home again?

You can't go
home again
because things
change and not
always for the
better.

There are
always changes
in the place

you once knew.
The place
where you
spent so many
happy carefree
days and
years.

I stood
outside the
gate and
recognized
nothing.

It was no
longer the
place where I
grew up. It no
longer
belonged to
me.

It bore no
resemblance to
happier times.

Tears gathered
in my eyes
because I'd
lost it all.

My feet were
immovable as
if cemented.

My heart felt
heavy.

Everything had
changed.

Where there
was joy now
stood anger
and
desperation.

Bodies move,
but not in
sync.

Faces look on
without
smiles.

Cleanliness
replaced by
filth.

No skipping
rope or
climbing
trees.

No hopscotch
or Hula-hoop.

No more
sitting on the
steps, looking
up at a starry
night.

No more
childhood
laughter while
playing house
with your best
friend.

Just don't try
to go home
again. You
won't like
what you see.

You won't like
what you hear.

Disappointment
reigns.

Storm clouds
set in.

Lips smile,
tears flow,

memories of
times long
past can't be
taken away, so
I walk away
with a smiling
mouth and a
floodtide of
memories in
tow.

I can't go
home again.

How green is
your grass

Are you rich?

How do you
categorize
your status?

How do you
measure your
wealth?

Is it by how
much money you
have? How many
friends you
have? How much
land you own
or your family
life?

I like to
think your
family life is
your best
life.

It's not how much money you have. That can go in the blink of an eye, and like the domino effect, false friends will fade quickly.

Land is forever, but will it always be yours?

You didn't ask for your siblings. They were just given to you, and they're not always trustworthy. They too can turn on you when expectations are not met. What now?

Nothing is
guaranteed.
Your spouse
will leave if
expectations
are not met.

Most children
expect
something,
depending on
your status.
They too can
turn on you.

What now?

Be your true
self, and the
rest will
follow. You
may be loved.
You may be
disliked, but
you will be
able to live
with who you
are.

When all is
said and done,

you are judged
by the company
you keep. If
you fly with
crows, you
will always
chatter and
eat rotted
meat. If you
fly with
doves, you
will be humble
and avoid the
chatter.

If you are
loved, then by
being your
true self,
your grass
will be
greener.
You'll be
loved for who
you are, not
what you are
or what you
have or don't
have.

Imperfection

Sometimes
there's beauty
in
imperfection
if you look
hard enough.
Nothing is
perfect. No
one is
perfect. Even
the most
perfect
looking flower
has flaws if
you look hard
enough to find
it, but the
imperfection
can be the
most beautiful
thing you've
ever seen
because it's
one of a kind.

A celebration
of women

There's
nothing more
rewarding than
celebrating a
hard-earned
achievement.

Over the years
women have
achieved so
much. Some we
know about and
some we don't.

On this day,
we gather to
celebrate the
strength and
resilience of
women. We
won't back
down. We won't
give up!

Women who
realize that
without
strength and
commitment
they are
heading for a
fall of great
magnitude.
Women who
realize that
without each
other, they
walk alone.
The road to
success is
never easy,
but they push
on through
darkness into
light.

We may
stumble, but
we don't fall,
and if we do
fall just a
little, we
rise up again,
stronger than

ever to take
our place in
this harsh
world of
naysayers and
doubters.

We are always
willing to
pass the torch
to those who
show the
courage,
determination,
and
willingness to
go forth into
a wasteland,
carrying life
and giving
water where
there was no
growth,
planting the
seed of life
to watch it
grow and
prosper.

We join hands
and hearts and
move mountains
and obstacles
to pave the
way for others
to achieve
even greater
things.

We tear down,
we rebuild, we
create, we
stand tall.

We love, we
trust, we
encourage. We
are the
forever people
who should be
celebrated
every day of
every year.

Let's raise
our glasses.
To US. To the
future! To
greatness! To
women!

Trash

Trash will be
trash, and the
only thing you
can do with
trash is
delete it from
your life— no
matter how you
dress it up,
it will still
be trash.
Hell! just
throw it in
the garbage.